The Steering Wheel Poems

by ELIZABETH DOYLE SOLOMON

Elizabeth Doyle Solomon

Cedar Creek Publishing
Virginia, USA

Cedar Creek Publishing
Bremo Bluff, Virginia
www.cedarcreekauthors.com

Printed in the United States of America

Library of Congress Control Number 2010940897

ISBN 978-0-9842449-8-0

Cover Photos

Photography is a hobby of Elizabeth's husband Bill, but represents both their loves and interests in back roads, mountains, forests, wildflowers, individual trees, butterflies, and old cabins.

Often taken from the steering wheel, the photos compliment and enhance the poems. Indeed, the world is a poem, and a photograph.

For my Grandmother
Florence Farley Doyle

For my Mother
Elizabeth Magdalene Fisher Doyle
Who died at thirty-nine

For my Father
Paul Farley Doyle, Sr.

Acknowledgments

- To my husband, Bill, who encouraged me.
- To the Friday poets in my home who listened to me.
- To Leonard Tuchyner who computerized these pages.
- To the Blue Ridge Chapter of the Virginia Writers Club
        who also encouraged me.
- To Linda Layne, of Cedar Creek Publishing,
        who believed in my work enough to publish
        this collection.

To God, by whose inspiration I have written.

Advance Reviews for
The Steering Wheel Poems

"Elizabeth Doyle Solomon's poems are love letters with a passion for nature and family. Her clear voice reaches deep into the music and rhythms of the natural world as it sings of such things as a hawk's tail writing on autumn skies and galloping spring-flooded streams. It bristles with a lover's protest at earth scraped raw in the name of progress.

The heart of this collection is rich with family memories: Mama's fragile strength, Daddy's playful Irish brogue, Grandma, who faced sorrow by giving grief to the prairie winds. Their courage and wisdom speak to us still in the poignancy and joy of Elizabeth's poems."

– SUNDAY ABBOT
Award Winning Poet
Poetry Society of Virginia

"Elizabeth Solomon is a brilliant poet. She possesses a facility with language that leaves prose writers simply marveling in her wake. Her secret? She writes, unhesitantly, from the heart–a warm heart that's experienced much of life's happiness, and an overgenerous helping of its woes. Your heart, no doubt, will respond."

– RICK BRITTON
Author & Historian
Jefferson, A Monticello Sampler

"Elizabeth's poetry bubbles forth from a total mind-body commitment to the craft. Though she produces at a phenomenal rate, each and every one of her poems feels hand-crafted, polished with loving care, and as rich as dark word chocolate. Regardless of what style or genre of poetry you normally enjoy, Elizabeth's poems hold something for everyone, and are meant to be read with the same loving care and smiles that have been placed into them. Read slowly; read carefully; read them one at a time, and you will be rewarded with great poetry, and your own (perhaps poetic) inspiration."

– JACK TRAMMELL
Author – *Down on the Chickahominy*

Table of Contents

Introduction

The Steering Wheel collection of poems came to be on the steering wheel of my Honda along the back roads of Albemarle, Greene, Orange, and Louisa counties. As has been my habit since age sixteen, I carry a journal every place I go. I've lost count at age sixty-seven, but I know there are over one thousand of them.

My poems have always come all at once. What to do while commuting two hours a day to teach school, tutor private students, or deliver newspapers? I found that if I could write the first two lines conceived, journal propped on the steering wheel—then later I could retrieve the rest on a parking lot, on a farm lane, or at home.

Some of these steering wheel poems have already been published in poetry magazines or anthologies. I give these acknowledgments, where due, at the book's end.

Long ago in my native New Orleans, Mama predicted when I was eight years old, that I'd be a writer. Those early scribbles on the backs of old envelopes were my first attempts. You were right, Mama.

THE STEERING WHEEL POEMS

I move past frozen farmland
steering wheel warm in my hands,
see Cooper's hawk perched beneath
perfect V's of honking geese—
all of us here just on lease.

CHANGES

Katydids have gone
wherever katydids go
out of themselves
leaving their skins below.

Crickets have arrived
doing their creaky hum;
soon summer will go
and winter must come.

A POEM IS

a rope I climb to possibility
seeds planted in my mind

wind to sail imagination's ship
window to soul, door to world

a breath of what I know
passage to understanding.

EVENSONG

Twilight stitches dark seams
against a smoky sky
a piece of pink peeking
from the west.

Gray gathers like smocking
pinched puffs of clouds
on a child's nightgown
as day is put to bed.

In a wink the light goes
to the earth's dark side
as we sing evensong
with the mockingbird.

PERFECT PEACE

I had lunch beside four horses
and a dozen Canada geese;
both the pasture and placid pond
were a portrait of perfect peace.

First yellow sulphur butterfly
sipped blue veronicas' honey;
what need did gentle creatures have
of new houses, cars, or money?

I watched the horses grazing grass,
geese paddling slow on the pond;
a Cooper's hawk as it glided
into unbroken blue beyond.

DESSERT

The sunset serves me
a dish of pastels,
colors so delicious
I can barely drive.

I spoon them
to my mind's page,
a dessert of words.

AUTO TEARS

Junked car, headlights gone
wires dangling from sockets
automobile tears.

THE SIGN

"Old man for hire"
sign hung on a wire
"odd jobs" it said
I could see his head

a shock of white hair
bending down there
working the soil
familiar with toil.

Wond'ring as I passed,
did he outlast
his old woman mate?
He leaned on a gate

and I saw the want,
in his eyes the taunt
thrown to desire—
old man for hire.

LIGHTING THE GLOOM

I gulp winter's air
as one starved for sun,
too many days of gray
frozen feet and face.

Then it happens—
mild January thaw
that upturned earth
rich loamy scent

and memories come
of Gulf Coast breeze
fragrance of jasmine
and gardenias

hibiscus flowers
bright scarlet petals
sun lighting the gloom
warmth thick as wild honey.

BIRDSONGS IN THE CAR

On this late August day
I drive through rain
listen to a program of
birdsongs, a walk through
woods in my car.

Each song recalls the
exact spot where I first
identified that bird.
From my bedroom at
Shamrock Ridge Farm

the whippoorwill
sang me to sleep.
At Silver Lake in New
Hampshire, I first heard
the tremolo of a loon.

But it was Llanarth Farm
woods on the James River
which gave me hundreds more:
owls, wrens, warblers, finches,
raptors and woodpeckers.

On this late August day
the years unpeel, layers
of an onion which bring
tears for the beautiful
birdsongs in my life.

MORNING WONDER

The morning road is thick
with mist, a world quietly
waking. Suddenly blue-gray
wings, long yellow legs lift
from the creek.

With effortless grace
great heron announces
his presence, minnows
scattered in minutes
before he rises.

Heron becomes my hymn
of morning praise
that in this warring world
there is still such
peaceful majesty, wonder.

CONSIDERING COWS

Black velvet beef machines
graze the yellowing maze
of February fields,
briefly stop their eating
to birth babies, exact
copies of themselves.

I used to slice their meat
with bone-handled knives
and cook what was left
of these beautiful ones—
broiled, stewed, fried
ground or pounded round
and think nothing of it.
But the methane they expel
tells a warning tale
of earth's warming
and I am filled with
a mix of chemicals.

I cannot pass a pasture
where the placid gassers
chew cuds without picturing
their awful slaughter.
Too slowly and too late
I've become a vegetarian.

EVERYWHERE IS GOING

Smoke rises from the pile
poisons tongues, lungs, air
where weeks before trees
purified, glorified earth.

Useless to cry, I drive by,
ask the Great Who to forgive.
I cannot. Everywhere is going;
nowhere is not a nice place to live.

HIGH COURT DECISION

Eleven million gallons
spilled into Prudhoe Bay
and only one week's profit
the company had to pay

for all the business lost
for the marine life killed
for all the tourism gone
when the crude oil spilled.

Those who sit on the high court
could never know the pain
the wildlife suffocated
from oil, slime and stain.

A mere slap on the hand
for polluting the seas:
the world's growing greedier,
more corrupt by degrees.

PROGRESS

Giant yellow jaws crunched, cracked
an acre of forest, splintered
in minutes a century's work.

Turning away did not stop the
sounds. Crr-ack! Tall white oaks
transformed into toothpicks.
Crr-unch! Old cedars disconnected,
roots thick as elephants' legs.

Stomach sickened, beliefs battered
hopes shattered for man's eco-heart
when eyes caught the sign's words:
"Progress For Your Community."

THE WATCHERS

She watches from country store
as lumber, plumbing, and dump trucks
park to fill tanks and stomachs.

Red-tail hawk circles, lands
atop a pole, watches sparrows
peck in barnyard dirt.

Security camera watches
storage buildings on land
that used to be pasture.

Old farmer in overalls
watches his world dwindle,
one acre at a time.

NOISE-NEEDERS AND QUIET-SEEKERS

The noise-needers grow in numbers;
they cannot stand the quiet—
they congregate in cities,
don't like rural life. They've tried it.

They're bored with trees and creaking frogs,
with cricket calls and singing birds—
they long for crowds and concrete walks,
for rush of feet and buzz of words.

The quiet-seekers want the woods;
they're strengthened by peacefulness
of mountain streams and waterfalls,
silver sprays that sunbeams kiss.

They cannot tolerate the noise
of screaming siren, blaring horn—
but lay their heads upon soft moss
where sweet discoveries are born.

RAPPING THE WORLD

They rap the world,
whoever is near—
in obnoxious sounds
we don't want to hear:

Radios, boomboxes
sound systems blaring—
obscene screaming,
sadistic swearing.

How did we move
from music to this?
Give me <u>real </u>songs,
old classical bliss!

WORDS

Words wire us together
lines of love
loneliness
poems of passion
portraits of people
we've never met.

Rhymed and unrhymed
we shed our skins
expose connections
that make us one:
beneath facades
breathes the spirit
of our humanity.

SUNSETS

A thousand sunsets
none ever the same,
each with fire-glow
and a twilight flame

spread into pastels
and faded by dark—
sunsets in seconds,
God's signature mark.

SURVIVORS

She parked as close as she could get
to the strip of surviving green—
where everything grew as it should,
in the wild, undefiled, and clean.

But oh, what a sad view it owned,
of the trash-littered parking lot—
God's royal creations enthroned,
and this was the poor praise they got!

A ROW OF CEDARS

A row of cedars eighty years old
kept out the wind, the biting cold—
gave homes to birds, both food and cover,
inspired poems from this tree lover.

Then came new owners, "Let's build a fence;"
cut and burned cedars, smoke intense—
fence didn't stop wind nor biting cold
like all those cedars eighty years old.

Fence kept nothing in, kept nothing out;
caused death, destruction, despair, doubt—
how could such a barren, lifeless thing
replace these live trees and birds that sing?

WHEN CRICKETS SING INSIDE THE HOUSE

When crickets sing inside the house
and pears hang golden on the tree—
when walnuts bang upon the roof,
it's autumn for the squirrels and me.

When roadside stands put pumpkins out
with baskets of apples and squash;
when cornstalks darken in the field
and all the leaves are color-washed—

When yellows bloom beside the road
and chilly mists hang in the air;
when honking geese fly south in V's
and acorn cups are everywhere—

When lawns and wooded lanes are thick
with leaves that whisper to the shoe,
and only chickadees are left—
do you get sentimental too?

SUDDENLY THE SUN

Suddenly the sun
splits the slate sky
spreads sparkling fingers
rings each rugged tree
sings his silent song
into the weary morning
brings light-music.
I wing, lark ascending,
wonder how this star
so far away can play
the harp in my heart.

THIS EARTH I RIDE

This earth I ride
is a pied pony
back dappled
with shadows
and sunlight.
He breathes
tolerance, patience;
but if I abuse him
he snorts, rears,
throws me off.
I must be gentle
with my pony.

FIRST THERE WAS FOREST

First there was forest,
filled with furry things
walking, crawling, flapping wings;
rooted, seeded, growing trees
colonies of honey bees
a patch of land pure and green
streams gleaming inbetween.

Then came the sign that said,
"Site Preparation by I. M. Hartless."
In two weeks, site "Prepared,"
beyond redemption or repair;
furry things, flapping wings,
growing trees, honey bees—gone,
a scraped raw place to build upon.

Amazing how cold cash talks;
where forest grew now concrete walks
condos, cars, nursery stock
along the edges of parking lots.
Scenes repeated, green defeated
by hard, lifeless asphalt black
wherever heartless men attack.

NOTHING WORTH SAVING

Litter blooms among the broom-sedge
hedge of trash cast from car windows;
plastic bags, beer cartons live here
tangled turmoil of carelessness
pressed by wind, thrown and grown
into a landscape of laziness.

I imagine someone plants a sign:
"Picture your front yard like this."
—then wonder if maybe their own
lawns are similar, a generation
convinced the world's a garbage can,
disposable everythings, nothing
worth saving, not even earth.

WASTELAND

Another fencerow goes this morning,
old sleepy cedars dragged out of bed
by their heads, bulldozed together
with feet exposed, and then torched.

In their places orange flags, stitches
on incisions in bare red earth where
only pressure-treated posts will
stand with strands of barbed wire.

No weed will be allowed to grow,
not one stem or stalk as cover for
rabbit chased by fox, no cedar
berries for birds whose droppings
made these old trees grow long ago.

Who can explain this madness,
murdering strong, living things
so quickly and casually? The owner
might reply it is his right,
but he has created a wasteland.

PENNIES FROM MY FATHER

Everywhere I stopped today
on every parking lot,
gleaming in the sunshine,
a penny at each spot.

I collected six of these
and then another
when the song hummed,
one sung by my father.

"Pennies from heaven
don't always come with rain;
sometimes they come with sun
to take away our pain."

I knew at once Daddy sent
those pennies to remind me
no matter where I'd moved to,
his old words would find me.

AUTUMN

Soybeans have turned
mustard yellow
under a sky
of pearly clouds;
broom-sedge fields
redden the edges
of October's road.

Not a leaf or blade
remains the same
under Autumn's hand;
even the hawk's tail
writes in russet
across the day.

SOMETHING ABOUT SEPTEMBER

Something about September
evokes a sadness in me:
Mama's lively, laughing eyes
watching my birthday cake bake;
frosting she cooked on the stove
that hardened to small white peaks;
the box of thin wax candles
waiting in the kitchen drawer.

Those agile, fine-boned fingers
curled my hair with bobby-pins,
while her own raven-black waves
needed no more than a brush.
Perhaps this month carries grief
because I stifled it then—
childhood ambushed by August:

the house that held only tears
which falling leaves repeated;
closet full of Mama's clothes,
a void I could never fill.
On this last day of September
I remember who she was—
and what her death took away.

WHO WE ARE

No one in my Gulf Coast clan
ever told of the cold, but
they knew. Grandpa was weaned
on snow in upstate New York.
Grandma's lips cracked from
Kentucky's icy winds
and Colorado's bitter blasts.

Aunt Mary Katherine
cut her teeth in Vermont,
and all eleven babies
of Grandma's were born on
the Oklahoma prairie.

It is only I and a
handful of my fifty cousins
who have chosen to stay in
four-seasons states while
the rest suntan in Florida
and Louisiana.

Who are we, I ask? Do we
define ourselves anymore
by region, we who dissolved
into the melting pot
of millions?

Continued

We are the grandchildren
and great-grands of immigrants,
migrants ourselves moving
from one place to another.
With hands soft or calloused
we reach for the chalice,
and share the spirit of
our hard-won democracy.

FEBRUARY MEMORIES

February breeze
bears on its breath
earthy scents
of mud and mulch
leaf-litter and lime.

It trails memories
of puppy grunts
and goat-kids' stunts
somersaulting in fields
of purple nettle.

From buried past
tiller turns the soil
glistening with grubs
and worms squirming
in surprise.

Children's voices
chatter and squeal
chase each other
through the fields
where goats graze.

Continued

Smooth young hands
drop seeds of squash
beans and beets,
plant seed-potatoes
and onion sets.

My bearded husband
swings an axe
and the woodpile grows,
insurance against
the winter snows.

Yesterdays, pungent
as newly-mown grass
pass before me;
such are the joys
and burdens of memory.

DADDY'S WEARING OF THE GREEN

My Irish Daddy Doyle
folded a dollar bill
until it was the size
of a sparrow's leg—

Greenbacked buttonhole
ev'ry St. Patrick's Day,
woke us all for school
with a wee bit of brogue:

"Top of the mornin' to ya!"
Long after his death
I see that dollar bill,
hear the voice I so loved.

Happy St. Patrick's Day,
Daddy. I miss you.

LESSONS

The lessons from generation
to generation are these:
how to live and how to die.

Mama's clear voice three weeks
before she died, "I'm going to
heaven. Promise me that you'll
be strong, the little mother."
I was eleven years old.

Then Daddy's sobbing every night
in their double bed, rising each
morning for his three children,
going to work and living because
he loved life.

My words when he was eighty and
diagnosed with Alzheimer's, "I
don't want you to die!" And his
answer, "We all have to die, honey.
I'm not afraid. Don't you be either."

PRAIRIE WIND: FOR
MY OKLAHOMA GRANDMA

"Wind never stops on the prairie."
Grandma's words, bodiless birds,
whispered as wind whipped through
cottonwoods, spun dust devils,
made tumbleweeds of my hair.
I knelt by two small stones, felt
a hundred years melt, Gram's tears
for stillborn babe buried
two weeks after Celia Mae died.

Gram never talked of sorrow.
"Don't borrow yesterday's tears,"
her prairie philosophy.
Uncle Bill, one of eleven,
told her stories to me, of the
buggy-driving doctor who dared
the blizzard of nineteen-five,
whose black bag held no hope
for Celia, dying of diphtheria.

For sixty years the endless wind
swept over Oklahoma graves
the day I sat snapping beans
with Gram, eighty-six.
"Did you ever cry?" I asked her.
The snapping never stopped as
she replied, "I cried, child, yes.
But I wiped tears on my apron,
gave my grief to the prairie wind."

STREETLIGHT: A NEW ORLEANS MEMORY

Streetlight, city light, siren and horn
set the city stage where I was born;
steam boats, tug boats, ocean-going ships
rode the river. I rode Mama's hips.

Humid and hot, sticky Delta heat
on the buses where whites got front seat;
streetcars hummed past each house with a maid
while I sucked ice, read books in the shade.

Night jasmine bloomed a scent like perfume
when death took Mama with him too soon;
streetlight, city light, siren and horn
all muffled my sobs that August morn.

Katrina destroyed without pity
my New Orleans, my native city;
Mama gone, Daddy gone, streetlights too,
lakefront a sad, devastated view.

Duct-taped freezers, antiques on the street
in the humid-hot sweet-sticky heat;
red paint marks each house, smeared on the door,
where nothing but mold lives anymore.

Streetlights, fog horns, hurricane lamps,
tramps find homes under overpass ramps;
humid and hot in New Orleans heat,
where my memories live, sad and sweet.

JANUARY

In all the year, this first month is the worst,
such gloom on heels of merry holidays
to lock the forest in an icy glaze
and freeze the lake whose shores the rushes nurse.
Even kingfisher rattles his disgust,
flies overhead where food is locked below;
great blue heron has been forced to go
and I am left to walk the dog at dusk.

On these nights I relax by fire's glow,
recall the songs that March and April bring
when every eve'ning all the thrushes know
I wait to hear their flute-like voices sing.
Until then gray skies send ice and snow,
and thrushes wait wherever thrushes go.

DO NOT

Do not look too long at the virgin land
this spring, denuded, deflowered—
at the zenith of its loveliest time,
for surely you shall grieve as I.

Do not look at the signs offering sale
of all that is not theirs to sell—
money lovers have never understood
that the earth belongs to us all.

Do not try to tell them with your poems
how very heartless they've become—
they will only point to your land and house,
sweep it clean even while you sleep.

CASHIER

Her trials traveled her face,
no joy, just pain in place
of gladness. Sadness glared
as though she always compared
her life to those of ease,
who never said thanks or please.

I found her smile today
with words that simply said,
"You're good at what you do."
Her eyes shone suddenly proud,
a kind word from the crowd.

ACCIDENT

Stopped in a dash
on her ancestral path
she had no warning
this bright spring morning;
killed in a heartbeat
car caught those swift feet
and the fawn inside
when the young doe died.

STREAMS

The streams run wild today,
race with April rain along
earth's arteries. Chestnut
brown they gallop, snort,
and whinny; escape with
wrath to other paths,
unreined, unbridled, free.

THE END OF A DAY

Life leaps onward full of energy,
but I lag and drag, sometimes go
backwards, so tired at the end of
a day that I think I know what
death must feel like as it approaches.

Strange how I was always moving
forward toward death—but never
felt or recognized it until now.
It is the weight on my legs, on
my mind. It is the invisible lead
sinker God tethers to us at birth.

BEATEN

She sat in the old truck
puffing on a cigarette,
face etched with disgust.
Whatever innocence she had
was beaten out of her—
both eyes blackened, cheeks
swollen with crying. Anger
and helplessness bridged
the distance between us,
as the man who disfigured
her approached. Her body
stiffened as he got into
the driver's side, flicking
a red-hot ash out the
window where it fell to
the indifferent asphalt.

A FIELD OF RYE

Like a man's brush-cut
rye rises even,
green stems the same height.

From such a small seed
it has all it needs
packed tightly within.

Type, timing and taste
with minimum waste,
small teacher of men.

RHYTHMS

Old man in a brown truck
chewed his tobacco plug.
His jaws swayed side to side
while a long coal train
passed near him on the track.
Cars swayed side to side,
one rhythm riding
beside the other.

LESSONS FROM SPARROWS

The sparrows have set up condos
in eaves of a convenience store;
they watch the SUV's and Hondas
as gas prices rise more and more.

But sparrows needn't worry;
their fuel's in worms and bugs,
or anything the shoppers drop
as they give disgusted shrugs.

They could teach us everything
about living the simple pace:
build your house with what you have,
be good to the folks in your space.

Broadcast your cheer rain or shine;
don't complain about bills to pay.
Be like the sparrows in condos,
who always have nice things to say.

THE WEATHER WITCH

There's a weather witch in the sky
who shakes her watering-hand
on only one side of the road
but leaves the sun where you stand.

Listen and you'll hear her chuckle
when roads for a mile are wet—
but because she's witching today,
the others aren't showered yet.

Some say it's because the devil
is busy beating his wife—
I say that the scattered showers
prove a weather-witch's life.

SUMMER'S HARVEST

I love the way summer bakes
into golden loaves of hay—
laid out on those oven-fields,
food supply for winter's stay.

So did I prepare my shelves.
I jellied, canned, and pickled—
four-foot critters were well-fed;
my family plump and tickled!

MUSCLED MAN

Muscled man in wide-brimmed hat
sat drinking malt liquor quarts
in the supermarket shade. Laid-back
slacker had no plans this June noon,
just guzzled the brew as summer blew
part of his life away.

DARE TO DEFY

The field of redtop grass
has a common mind and will,
bends which way the wind blows,
knows only the status quo.
So too with people who bend
the most comfortable way,
never dare to be different,
choose the easiest path.

Weak-stemmed grasses pose
for artist's brush, inspire
pens and lens. Give me, rather,
the leathery oak, muscled limbs
trim from fighting wind, snow,
and ice—who dares to stand
defiant on his storm-tossed crest.

RED-TAILED HAWK

On broad silent wings he flies
three feet above my head from
left to right across the road,
fluted red tail catching sunset's
swale, his mission of one mind
to find the hapless mouse who
runs from nest to field, yields
a meal for the sharp-eyed hawk.

THE GIFT

Up the steep slope he crawled
belly close to the ground
fluffy red tail half his length
then stopped, turned, pointy ears
tuned to our steps, dog and I,
sat on his haunches, stared.

Against the bare dry clay where
land was cleared for a house,
curiousity caught the fox,
his silhouette framed against
the last glow of sunset sky,
a poem already written in mind,
the wild one's gift to me.

PASSING A GRAVEYARD

It's strange to say hello
to the dead who cannot hear—
their ashes, brittle bones
in the graveyard that's so near.

These monuments in stone,
brass markers with date and name—
are all that's left of life,
their silent and petty fame.

Don't plant me in the ground
as though I were bush or tree—
give my ashes to the wind
that scatters me wild and free.

MAN

Man is a comma
in eternity's book,
one blink of an eye
when millions look—

and yet he rises
immeasurable soul
to be part of God,
and so become whole.

About the Author

Elizabeth Doyle Solomon and husband, Bill

Elizabeth Doyle Solomon was christened Elizabeth Ann Doyle in the autumn of 1942 in New Orleans, Louisiana. She was called "Betty Ann," to distinguish her from Mama, also Elizabeth, who was called Betty.

Elizabeth's very first poem was selected by the nuns at the St. Mary of Angels Catholic School when she was twelve years old, just after her mother died. It represented this K-8 school at a district contest.

Marriage brought her to the mountains of West Virginia where she lost two babies and adopted two infant daughters. The years brought her to Virginia where she edited "The Rhyme's Den" poetry column in the *Winchester Evening Star*. She then founded and became editor of the *Central Virginia Leader* newspaper in the early 1980's. Her local poetry column in the *Leader* was called "The Poets' Tree," and she wrote hundreds of weekly columns about wildflowers, trees, and butterflies in "Back Roads."

Along the way, she found time to take care of thirty-five foster children from ages one week to nineteen years old. In 1985, Agape Press published her first collection of poems, *SEASONS*, in her native Louisiana. It followed the seasons of the year, and had wildflower and nature illustrations by local Albemarle artist Ana Maria Liddell.

Elizabeth did not submit any poems to poetry journals until the year 2003. The press of returning to college at age fifty-two and subsequent years of teaching and tutoring as a single woman prevented anything except what her profession demanded. These last seven years have been a gift to herself. Elizabeth has received numerous awards from the Poetry Society of Virginia (for which she also served as Contest Chair), and from the Blue Ridge Chapter of the Virginia Writers Club. As a K-4 teacher, she has conducted poetry workshops in the classroom for over thirty-five years. She has moderated a poets' critique group every week since 2003 for the Virginia Writers Club.

Elizabeth's poems and articles have been published in *Albemarle Almanac*, *Charlottesville Observer*, *From Riverbanks to Mountaintops Anthology*, *Mid-America Poetry Review*, *Appalachian Voice*, *Nomad's Choir*, *Pegasus*, *A Common Wealth of Poetry*, *Red Owl*, *Blue Ridge Anthology 2007 and 2009*, *The Louisiana Review*, *Westward Quarterly*, *Poesia*, *Timber Creek Review*, *The Lyric*, and *Plainsongs*.

Elizabeth and her two rescued cats.

From New Orleans to West Virginia, from northern to central Virginia, Elizabeth's journey has led her to a country road in Albemarle County, Virginia, where she shares a book-filled home with her husband Bill, a black Persian cat named Shadow, and two rescued cats—Emily Dickinson II ("Em") and Robert Frost ("Bob-Cat").

Her next collection has already begun, a group of memoir pieces called *Journey West—and Everywhere*. She looks forward to meeting you again there.

JUL -- 2011

Breinigsville, PA USA
29 November 2010
250224BV00002B/3/P